C000195936

AROUND
LOUTH
IN OLD PHOTOGRAPHS

Looking over the roof tops of Louth c. 1952.

AROUND
LOUTH
IN OLD PHOTOGRAPHS

COLLECTED BY
DAVID CUPPLEDITCH

ALAN SUTTON
1989

Alan Sutton Publishing
Gloucester

First published 1989

Copyright © 1989 David Cuppleditch

All rights reserved. No part of this publication may be reproduced, stored in a retrieval system, or transmitted, in any form or by any means, electronic, mechanical, photocopying, recording or otherwise, without the prior permission of the publishers and copyright holder.

British Library Cataloguing in Publication Data

Around Louth in old photographs.
1. Lincolnshire. Louth, history
I. Cuppleditch, D.
942.5'32

ISBN 0-86299-702-X

Typesetting and origination by
Alan Sutton Publishing
Printed in Great Britain by
Dotesios Printers Limited

CONTENTS

INTRODUCTION

Most Ludensian historians have used photographs sparingly in their researches. Instead they have relied heavily on 'the written word' and this has left a noticeable gap in Louth's long and illustrious history. There are many errors in the spoken word whereas photographs rarely lie.

According to Richard Goulding, William Armitage was the first to experiment with daguerreotypes in Louth. Armitage, an inventor (1814–49), was also a pioneer in developing fog signals for the railway and something of an eccentric. His untimely death was recorded in the *Annual Register* of 1849:

> About three o'clock in the afternoon a melancholy accident took place in the town of Louth in Lincolnshire, by which 5 persons were killed. The unfortunate deceased were Mr William Armitage, a chemist and inventor of fog signals for railways, his father, his housekeeper and a boy and girl employed by him. It appears that Mr Armitage had received a large order for signals, which was to be completed and the signals delivered at Doncaster on Monday morning. Being pushed for time he endeavored to dry the detonating materials used in the signals with unusual speed. Over the kitchen was a wareroom in which the father and the boy and girl, who also perished, were at work. Mr Armitage placed 50 of his signals in the oven and having done so left the place for a short time. On his return, the housekeeper who was with a maidservant in the kitchen, told him she thought the oven was getting too warm. He went to ascertain the fact and on opening the door of the oven the combustable materials within exploded with such violence that a portion of the premises became a heap of ruins. The body of Mr Armitage was found, shockingly mutilated on the further side of a pantry adjoining the kitchen, having been driven through the partition wall by the force of the explosion. The father and the girl were quite dead when extricated from the ruins. The boy, who was with them in the wareroom, only survived an hour, his limbs having been frightfully scorched and blackened. The housekeeper was dreadfully mutilated by the falling in of the upper portion of the building consequent upon the explosion. She like the boy was taken out alive and was able to state before she died how the accident happened; she also mentioned that she had several times remonstrated with Mr Armitage on the impropriety of his drying his signals in the oven, but had only been laughed at by him for her warnings. The maidservant who was in the kitchen at the time appears to have had a miraculous escape, having been blown out through the window into the yard. Besides the 50 signals which exploded and caused such fearful destruction, there were on the premises hundreds more, which happily escaped.

It was left to Joseph Willey, Louth's first established photographer, to explore the possibility of the medium and he made a handsome living from his craft. Later photographers such as Plumtree, Clarence and Arthur James cashed in on the craze as photographs became popular. One of the most interesting of these latter day Victorians was Joseph Matthews who took over Alexandra Studios in Ramsgate from Clarence James. When Matthews died all his glass plates were stored in a garden shed on the Keddington Road. After 50 years of neglect his grandson retrieved them only to find that the majority of the images had rotted away through damp, mould and infestation. I have included some of the printable photographs in this book.

Perhaps the most celebrated photographer in Louth was Arthur James of Ramsgate House, who after a busy career had to sit back and watch all his equipment and indeed his lifetime's work float down Ramsgate in the disastrous flood of 1920. At the turn of the century every town in Lincolnshire had its own photographer and they quickly became part of the social scene. In Alford there was Nainby, in Lincoln there was Slingsby, in Stamford there was Miss Higgins and so on. Each photographer had his own patch.

Old photographs are interesting social documents in themselves. They remind us what life was like, what interests people had and what previous generations looked like. There have been so many changes in recent years not least those caused by the present property boom that just looking at old buildings in Louth could take up a volume in itself. But the town is comprised of individuals and that is its strength. They are more important than their domiciles or the buildings where they once worked which is why I have included so many group photographs in this volume.

Ludensian architecture is easily followed through the Georgian, Victorian and Edwardian periods. However, the more recent additions from 1950 onwards may puzzle future generations.

For me, the most gratifying part of this book has been the section on the fifties as it is within most people's memory, although it is difficult to believe that the fifties are now part of history. In some ways it only seems like five minutes ago, in others it seems like a life time away.

There was a fervour for 'new' things in that post-war period. New meant clean, tidy and uncluttered and in this fervour which continued throughout the 1960s and '70s many so-called modern buildings were erected without much thought. One of the most recent examples is the monstrosity at the end of George Street on the site of the old George Hotel. There were other renovations, however, which blended in with their surroundings, such as the Bridge Street block of flats – a very run down building at one time, since returned to its former glory. In the main old-fashioned things were out of vogue, and not just in architecture – button back Victorian chairs were chopped up to keep the workman's braziers burning in Mawers yard while paintings considered worthless or even books were discarded on the 'Stones' (i.e. the Cornmarket auction sales) where they made very little money. It was the same with photographs but fortunately one or two caches were left to gather dust in people's lofts and attics and are gradually being rediscovered now.

The history of Louth is basically about people – their successes and their shortcomings. In this saga of provincial life where problems are sometimes blown up out of all proportion it is worth remembering that Louth has been a religious centre for the last thousand years, catering for all kinds of denominations.

The first record of Louth dates from the time of Edward the Confessor when the land in and around the Borough was valued at £12 – there has been a bit of inflation since then. And 'there was nowt wrong' with the rebellion in Louth when locals were so incensed by Henry VIII's clamp down on the monasteries and religious institutions that they were prepared to take up arms against him in 1536.

The rebellion fizzled out and the vicar of Louth was hanged, drawn and quartered for his troubles.

Nearly a hundred years later Louth was badly hit by the plague. In 1631 nearly 500 people died out of a population of just 1,000; trade was suspended and the town deserted. The great hero of that time was Sir Charles Bolle of Thorpe Hall, a physician who did much to suppress the disease. Undoubtedly Louth's greatest asset is its parish church. The spire of St James', the highest parish church spire in the land has tempted one or two people to climb it. In 1818 a cobbler called Benjamin Smith placed a bet that he could negotiate the spire after drinking ten pints of ale. He did too, danced a hornpipe on the top stone and then descended only to find that the person with whom he had placed his bet had absconded with the money.

During this century many famous people have visited Louth, including General Booth of the Salvation Army, Lord Baden-Powell of the Boy Scout movement, John Betjeman (the late poet laureate and great friend of Jack Yates) and Mahatma Gandhi. The last of these was perhaps the most surprising. Gandhi came to Louth twice; the first time in 1906 when he stopped with his friend Mr West of Aswell Street and the second time two years later. West first met Gandhi in South Africa at a vegetarian restaurant in Johannesburg. West had gone there in 1902 as a printer's representative and the two men were to correspond throughout their lives.

In the Second World War much of the country's 'top brass' visited Louth. General Montgomery flashed through the town and General Horrocks was based here for a short time but the most surprising visitor was Winston Churchill who stopped overnight; his visit was as brief as it was secret in those early days of the war.

More recently the Louth MP Jeffrey Archer, who succeeded Cyril Osborne, has gained much notoriety as a fiction writer and Corinne Drewery of 'Swing Out Sister', a pop group, has generated much interest in the younger element of Louth. It is only when you talk to locals that you discover some surprising facts such as Mike Graves of Gospelgate going on a drinking binge with Errol Flynn in Spain or the tantrums of the tennis circuit from Mike Lugg when he was umpiring at Wimbledon. Another unexpected visitor to Louth in the fifties was Dr Donald Soper, the controversial cleric; while Geoff Capes, the Lincolnshire policeman has appeared many times in the eighties as a strong man personality.

Louth has always been a hospitable place catering for an assortment of characters. In the last century it welcomed Buffalo Bill Cody when his circus performed in a field off the Keddington Road with all the paraphernalia of his extraordinary showmanship. Even today the town still opens its doors to a constant stream of visitors and continues to act as host regardless of class, creed or sanity.

What has become apparent to me in compiling this book is not so much the quantity of photographers in Louth, and goodness knows there have been dozens, but the diversity of their styles. From Clare to Garland, Rawlings to Atterby and Towle to White, their interpretations have differed greatly.

Photographers still emerge and long may they continue to snap away. For their contribution which seems inconsequential at the time is part of the town's heritage and so part of Louth's history.

Up to the First World War

LINCOLNSHIRE HAS LONG BEEN AN AGRICULTURAL COUNTY. Haymaking in Grimoldby with St Edith's Church in the background is evocative of life at the turn of the century. Mr Vamplew is standing in the foreground with arms folded. (Postcard.)

ALSO IN GRIMOLDBY, these fine shire horses are pulling a John Cooke waggon. These were made at the Lindum Works, Lincoln and cost £40. (Postcard.)

THIS IS A DELIGHTFUL STUDY of the Smith sisters; Louise, Jenny and Nellie, of South Cockerington. The photograph was taken in the garden of The Hollies and is a typical informal Victorian composition. One of these three girls was to marry into the Needham family of farmers of South Cockerington. (A. Broadley.)

AT THE TURN OF THE CENTURY Louth Horse Fair was held on a much diminished scale since J.M.W. Turner's day when he painted Louth Horse Fair from Upgate. It was held twice a year when 'prospective nags' were put through their paces between Lee Street and Aswell Street on Newmarket although it was overshadowed by the bigger fairs held at Lincoln and Horncastle. (A. Broadley.)

THIS EARLY PHOTOGRAPH of the Market Place, Louth, from a badly kept glass plate, shows the old pump which many Ludensians used for their water. (It is possibly a Joseph Willey photograph.)

MERCER ROW, LOUTH.

IN THIS LATER POSTCARD of Mercer Row, showing the pump to the right of the picture, it is clear that one or two Louth tradesmen were not afraid of displaying their wares. I doubt whether present shopkeepers would be allowed to continue this practice of placing their merchandise in the street.

THIS PORTRAIT OF JOSEPH MATTHEWS (1862–1927) photographer, shows a man with astute qualities. He was the youngest child of a family of ten and was three years old when his father died. He initially trained as an artist at the Royal College of Art and exhibited at Newark and Nottingham (his name appears in the dictionary of British Artists) but at some stage gave up painting for photography. In 1881 he visited Canada and the USA. In 1891 he married Florence Brookes, the daughter of a piano maker of Muswell Hill, London. He settled in Louth a year later and took over Clarence James' Studio in Ramsgate.

'WHERE DID YOU GET THAT HAT?' In this group shot, the ladies have excelled themselves with their headgear, which makes me think it might be a family wedding. (Joseph Matthews.)

HERE WE SEE THE BLUSHING BRIDE. This single portrait by Joseph Matthews reflects the occasion well with the bunch of flowers on her lap, contrasting with her silk dress. (Joseph Matthews.)

MATTHEWS OBVIOUSLY ENJOYED TAKING GROUP PORTRAITS. In this family photograph of a prosperous middle-class family (grandfather looks well fed) he had even managed to capture the family pet. (Joseph Matthews.)

THIS DELIGHTFUL PHOTOGRAPH of Florence Matthews (wife of Joseph) – under the umbrella – was taken between Abbey Park and Cowslip Lane, Keddington. On the bridle path we can see a group of children picking flowers. The photograph is dated 1896 and Harold (Joseph's son) is dressed in the sailor suit. (Joseph Matthews.)

IN THIS PHOTOGRAPH OF HUBBARDS HILLS it is possible to see why this idyllic beauty spot has been so popular over the years. Even in Victorian times it was serene. (P. & S. London.)

IN THE VICTORIAN ERA leisure time was a precious commodity. People took note of their free time and wanted to remember it. Here we see a group at Welton Vale. The lady fourth from the left (standing) was Mrs Vamplew; next to her, third from the left (also standing), was Mr Willman; while the tall moustached gentleman, ninth from the left (standing at the back) was Harry Rose who owned a cycle shop in Eastgate. Meanwhile the gentleman with the bowler hat, lying on the ground (to the left at the front) was Mr Furnish, the hairdresser, and the gentleman lying to the extreme right (front row) was Mr J. Lill. (F.A. White.)

QUEEN VICTORIA'S DIAMOND JUBILEE in 1897 was quite an event, to which nearly everyone in Louth turned out. Here we see the Mayor, Henry Simpson JP addressing schoolchildren in the Market Place. (A. James.)

TO MARK THE EVENT a bullock was roasted. Matthew Smalley is holding the ill-fated animal (1897).

THIS WAS THE VIEW of the Market Place in 1897. (A. James.)

THE WHOLE TOWN made an effort for the Jubilee celebrations. This rather faded print of the Ship & Horns by Joseph Matthews (1862–1927) shows an excess of arboreal decoration. Mr Hargraves (the owner) is standing in the doorway. (Joseph Matthews.)

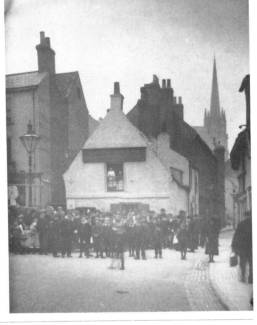

THE SHIP & HORNS had changed quite considerably under Mr James Hargraves. He had been given permission to knock down the old pub (seen here) and put an extra storey on his new hostelry, providing he relinquished a few feet to allow for a pavement to be built in Little Eastgate. (Joseph Matthews.)

MEANWHILE A MASSIVE FOUNTAIN was erected in the Cornmarket. This was a view of it with the Mason's Arms pub in the background. (Joseph Matthews.)

... AND THIS WAS another view of it looking the other way. (Joseph Matthews.)

THIS EARLY STUDY OF WINTER on the canal, taken by Joseph Matthews (c. 1890), shows that life could be a bit bleak. People had to make their own entertainment.

WHILE THIS EARLY PHOTOGRAPH OF LOUTH from the Grimsby Road portrays Louth as a sleepy backwater dominated by the spire of the parish church of St James'. (Plumtree.)

21

WHEREAS THORPE HALL on the Lincoln Road is one of the most impressive large houses in Louth. It even has its own ghost – a legendary 'Green Lady' who is said to haunt the Hall pining after Sir John Bolle who died in 1606. (Plumtree.)

THE LOUTH CONSTABULARY in 1892. Back row: PCs Barnard, Neal, Howsham, Ferriby, Cook, Peacock and Elvin. Front row: Sgt. Smith, Superintendant Barham and Sgt. Pridgeon.

AT THE TOP OF LEE STREET, next to Bowling Green Lane, there used to be a house (now demolished) where this charming informal portrait was taken. It was of Herbert Broadley who later worked for the Ministry of Food and Agriculture and subsequently did a spell with the United Nations. He was friendly with Dag Hammarskjold, (Secretary-General of the United Nations) and was knighted. He was also made a Freeman of the Borough of Louth. (A. Broadley.)

IN THIS PHOTOGRAPH OF THE CATTLEMARKET it is just possible to see the Broadley family home in the far distance.

THIS PHOTOGRAPH BY A. James shows the proclamation of Edward VII as King on 29 January 1901.

THIS WAS THE HOUSE on the side of the cattlemarket where Herbert Broadley was born. The clearly visible sign states that his father was a wheelwright, joiner, painter and undertaker. The name is perpetuated today in Broadley Crescent. (A. Broadley.)

MOST MIDDLE-CLASS FAMILIES IN LOUTH had a maid. She would fetch and carry, do the cooking, tidy the house and, in fact, take care of all the unwanted chores that everyone detested. This was a maid, the unsung heroine of Victorian society and this informal snapshot showed she could be pretty too. (A. Broadley.)

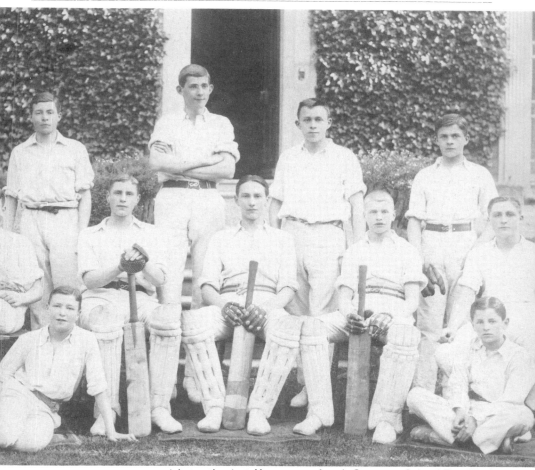

HERBERT BROADLEY was a cricket enthusiast. Here we see Louth Grammar School First XI of 1910 with both the Broadley brothers on the photograph. From left to right (back row): H. Surgey (whose father was vicar of Muckton), H. Strawson, Herbert Broadley and Alec Broadley. Front row: L. Sawyer, J.S. Genney, J. Ward, A. Taylor (capt.), A. Ward, P. Evison and A. Stubbs. (A. James.)

LINCOLNSHIRE HAS ALWAYS produced characters and eccentrics. This was Tommy Locking who had a shop in Church Street, Louth.

IT WOULD SEEM that one of Tommy Locking's pleasures in life was to give small children and dogs a ride on his home-made cart. He was a sort of latter day Victorian children's entertainer. This photograph was probably taken at Carlton.

COMFORTABLE FOOTWEAR was important and at the turn of the century boots were fashionable. Mr Smith (seen here) was a manager at Stead & Simpson's in Sudbury, Suffolk before opening his own shoe shop in Upgate, Louth. In 1912 the business moved to Mercer Row where the Smith family were to sell boots and shoes for the next 70 years.

THIS WAS THE WEDNESDAY CORNMARKET when a variety of objects were put on sale. There were auctions and stallholders and plenty of welcoming hostelries. Of the pubs that existed then the Crown & Woolpack, the Crown & Sceptre, Mason's Arms Vaults, Bodega, B.Y.B. Vaults and the Waterloo have gone. Only the Mason's Arms Hotel is left and even its future is uncertain. (Postcard c. 1900.)

THE LOUTH BRITISH SCHOOL under the headmastership of Mr Trewick (the moustached gentleman on the right of this photograph). The British School is now known as Kidgate.

THE YOUNG BOY in the centre of this photograph on a 'Safety' bicycle was Percy Latter who was eventually to become the headmaster of Kidgate School. The cycle craze swept through Britain and helped to establish the firm of Raleigh, although there were many other makes such as Gun, Hercules and Hillman, Herbert and Cooper to name but a few. (A. James.)

THE POPULARITY OF THE CYCLE CRAZE soon led to races. Here we see a group of Louth cyclists about to compete in a cross-country race.

THE INTRODUCTION OF MOTORIZED WAGONS presented several problems: they were cumbersome, awkward and smelly. Here we see C.G. Smith's steam wagon in some difficulty on Alford Hill. It was driven by Mr Trolley who lived in Upgate.

THIS WAS C.G. SMITH'S SHOP FRONT in Upgate (demolished in 1976) where they sold all manner of soaps and detergents. Louth carbolic, their most famous product, was manufactured at the back of the shop in what is now known as Church Close. (A. James.)

THE DAYS OF CANAL TRAFFIC were numbered. This picture of a coal barge slowly meandering up the Louth Canal at the turn of the century is evocative of another age – even then. (Liza Finney was the owner of the barge.) It is just possible to see the two churches in the same churchyard at Alvingham in the distance.

EVE AND RANSHAW continued with their team of four shire horses to pull their waggons. This photograph taken at the junction of Horncastle Road with Edward Street shows South Street House in the background.

JUST AROUND THE CORNER, George Street in 1880 looked much the same as it does today. Gone are the gas lamps and the tower from the 'tower house' but it still retains much of its charm.

THESE NEW GOTHIC REVIVAL BUILDINGS were erected in 1869 in place of the old Georgian buildings in School House Lane as part of Louth Grammar School. Old boys of the Grammar School have included: Capt. John Smith of Pocahontas fame and founder of Virginia; Franklin the Arctic explorer; John Eyre after whom Lake Eyre and the Eyre mountains were named and of course Alfred Lord Tennyson the Victorian Poet Laureate. (A. Broadley.)

THAT AUGUST BODY known as Louth postmen taken by photographer A. James in around 1905. Postmaster Reed (sixth from left seated in the front row) was in charge and of the others it is possible to identify: Rawlings, Ruffel Ward, Gowing, Bell, Barton, Johnson, Hempstock, Mee, Catchpole, Warne, Patrick, Auested, Clark, Erriman, Goodhall, Wilson, Brewer, Carter, Reed, Wilson, Donner and Borman. Whitworth (third from right) became postmaster at Windsor.

LIEUT.-GENERAL ROBERT BADEN-POWELL paid a visit to Louth Grammar School in July 1900 to donate a bust which he had had made of his ancestor Captain John Smith. He inspected the Cadet Corps, opened a new gymnasium and presented prizes in Louth Town Hall. Baden-Powell has always been credited as the defender of Mafeking and founder of the Boy Scout movement; but he was also an accomplished watercolour artist. He sketched and painted throughout his life, working for a short spell on *The Graphic* newspaper under a pseudonym. He was Honorary Vice President of The London Sketch Club until his death.

HERE WE SEE Baden-Powell inspecting a group of Boy Scouts in Hubbards Hills.

SHOWING ALL THE TRAPPINGS of a successful architect, here we see Major and Mrs Fowler together with their chauffeur Mr Alfred Otley. James Fowler (1828–92) was responsible for much of Louth's Victorian architecture and did much to restore churches in and around Louth. (A. James.)

FOWLER WAS RESPONSIBLE for the restoration of St James' in 1868. The interior of St James' is spacious and striking with parts of it made up from the original thirteenth-century materials. Since this photograph was taken the pulpit has been transferred to the other side of the aisle and the gas mantles have gone.

ST JAMES' CHURCH has been lucky with its organists: George Porter was organist from 1866–98 and Owen Price from 1898–1946. The present organist and choirmaster is Peter Burness. George Porter (seen here) lived in Church Close, Westgate and was responsible for the success of Louth Choral Society which still flourishes today.

THIS TRANQUIL PICTURE of the Revd Surgey with his wife and two sons, Monty and Gordon, was taken at Muckton Rectory, near Louth. Monty Surgey features on the earlier cricket photograph of Louth Grammar School First XI of 1910.

GOULDING'S BOOKSHOP IN MERCER ROW was old-fashioned and Dickensian (J.W. Goulding is standing in the doorway). They were responsible for producing *Goulding's Almanack* which ran for many years. All the printing took place on the top floor of their premises. After the demise of Gertrude Goulding the printing machines were transferred to the back of the shop where Mr Houghton continued to print selected books and memorabilia until his death.

THE GOULDING DAUGHTERS Annie (left) and Gertrude (right) continued to run the bookshop for many years after their parents' death. Gertrude Goulding eventually died in 1948.

THIS PHOTOGRAPH OF JOHN WILLIAM GOULDING, printer and bookseller, and his wife was taken in the garden of No. 28 Gospelgate. They were the parents of Richard Goulding (1868–1929) Louth's most celebrated local historian.

THE TURK'S HEAD (c. 1900) on the corner of Aswell Street with Queen Street has not changed a great deal. Mrs King (the lady with her hand on the window sill) was the licensee. The other ladies were (from left to right): Mrs Stanley, Mrs King's niece, her small son and Mrs Wilson and –?–.

THERE WAS A TIME when Lincolnshire could boast of its large country houses. Sadly in this century many of them have been demolished. Walmsgate Hall was just one of the victims.

FORMERLY THE HOME of the Dallas-Yorkes and latterly the home of Mr Haggas, Walmsgate Hall was built c. 1835. It was particularly noted for its Italian gardens (a feature known for miles around) and needed seven full time gardeners to keep it in trim.

DALLAS-YORKE NARROWLY MISSED being part of the Charge of the Light Brigade through illness. He did, however, still ride to hounds when he was in his nineties. His daughter, the beautiful Winifred Dallas-Yorke went on to marry the Duke of Portland.

ANOTHER CASUALTY OF Lincolnshire's fine old country houses was Bayon's Manor in Tealby. Built by Charles Tennyson d'Eyncourt, the wealthy lawyer and uncle of Alfred, Lord Tennyson, it smacked of Victorian opulance and pretentiousness. Nevertheless it was still a shame when the ruinous house was blown up in the early '60s. There is a particularly fine portrait of Charles Tennyson d'Eyncourt in Louth Town Hall which was presented by Robert Ranshaw in 1904. Charles Tennyson D'Eyncourt was High Steward for Louth from 1836 to 1862.

THERE HAD BEEN A CASTLE on this site built by Bishop Odo of Bayeux, half brother of William the Conqueror. But the building which Charles Tennyson built turned the much smaller Tealby Lodge (where his father lived) into a monstrous folly. Like adopting the d'Eyncourt to the end of his surname, he was allowed to wallow in medieval grandeur on a scale only possible in Victorian England.

IN ITS HEYDAY Elkington Hall was the home of W.G. Smyth. During the First World War Lord Wilton lived there and latterly it was home of the Dobson family before it was demolished. (Hickingbottom & Bullomore of Lincoln.)

THIS FAMILY PARTY of the Smyth clan was taken on 6 September 1900 by the photographer Arthur H. Whinfield: W.G. Smyth, the venerable old captain, seated in the centre of the group complete with fez was a true eccentric but well-liked by the people of Louth.

A GROUP OF SERGEANTS from the Louth Volunteers in around 1870. Sergeant Furnish is on the extreme left of the picture and the only other discernable face is that of Sergeant Weaver. The Royal Garrison Artillery Volunteers were formed against the background of much table-thumping and sword-rattling by Napoleon III in the 1860s. (Plumtree.)

FOR MANY YEARS the Volunteer Arms in Northgate was the only reminder of those troubled times in the last century when the French posed a threat. Sadly the Volunteer Arms has been demolished, as indeed has the Wilde Hall a bit further down Northgate, to make way for a block of flats. (Edward Land.)

IN THIS EARLIER PHOTOGRAPH we see a much younger Capt. Smyth at the reigns. He was one of the first people to go caravaning for pleasure, possibly influenced by the Revd George Hall from Ruckland and author of *The Gypsy Parson*. W.G. Smyth converted his gypsy caravan and toured Britain long before the craze caught on.

COACH-BUILDERS ABOUNDED IN LOUTH. There were Richardsons, Esbergers and Thorns all making fine carriages for conveyance. Most of these coach-builders were situated off Chequergate and in the region of Spoutyard and Ludgate.

THE OLD HORSE AND TRAP was steadily replaced by motor vehicles. Here at the junction of Eve Street and Northgate we see Pratt's spirit wagon.

CHARLIE JOHNSON of No. 14 Little Eastgate took this photograph. His premises, currently occupied by Nicholson, Rushton & Smith, architects, was later taken over by George Stubbs, yet another photographer. The people in this photograph were: John Blyth, (the Louth town crier), John Taylor (the auctioneer) Mrs Col. Webb (Countess of Wilton) and Fred Smithson. The shop behind Fred Smithson was Ward's Grocers.

THIS WAS THE REVD STANFORD'S BOYS' BRIGADE in South Elkington dated 1910.

THE LOUTH VOLUNTEERS used to practise at the Cow Pastures near Elkington. Here we see a group of them in 1910 including Capt. Noel Faulkner and Capt. Worral parading outside Elkington Hall with Capt. Smyth (the old man with the overcoat, hat and beard) looking on. It is interesting that one officer and the sergeant-major are still wearing uniforms more applicable to the Boer War.

THIS DELIGHTFUL STUDY (photographer unknown) of a dancing class was taken in 1915 at South Elkington. These were the days before radio when groups of people made their own entertainment and when the wind-up gramophone with those heavy 78 records were quite a novelty.

LOUTH HAS ALWAYS BOASTED a fine choir and choral society. Here we see the choir in 1916 under the watchful gaze of Canon Lenton who left Louth in 1928 when he was appointed vicar of Hessle. (A. James.)

THIS GROUP MADE UP PART of the Palestine exhibition staged in 1906 by the choir and clergy of St James' Church.

ON CORONATION DAY 1911, there were many celebrations. This was the Royal Antediluvian Order of Buffaloes (326 Luda Lodge) at the White Hart in Aswell Street. Many leading Louth businessmen belonged to this select band. (W.E. Roberts.)

WHILE AT ELKINGTON there were also celebrations under the auspices of the Revd Stanford.

KENWICK HALL NEAR LOUTH was condemned during the Second World War after bombing had made the structure unsafe. The original Kenwick Hall was owned by the Allenby family and enlarged in 1889 by Cheney Garfit, the banker of Mercer Row. After it was pulled down another hall was built on the same site which for years was the home of Miss Diana Dixon.

EASTFIELD LODGE WAS NOT SO LUCKY. It was left derelict for many years and was only recently demolished. Here we see Major Allott and his beagles (c. 1920) in front of Eastfield Lodge on Keddington Road.

THE LOUTH SUFFRAGETTES gave Lloyd George a rough ride when he came to Louth to speak on 15 January 1910. As he spoke in Louth Town Hall he was heckled by members of the audience and one or two suffragettes dropped stink bombs on him from the rafters. Lloyd George beat a hasty retreat. (Postcard.)

DETAILS OF LLOYD GEORGE'S PRIVATE LIFE have only come to light in recent years. A male chauvanist by nature and a womanizer by inclination, his name was linked with the beautiful and sophisticated Mrs Timothy Davies (wife of the local Louth MP) who is seen here with her youngest son.

A TROOP OF CAVALRY going through its paces at Louth Camp in 1912 in preparation for the First World War. (Postcard c. 1912.)

THE SALVATION ARMY and before them the Temperance Society have always had strong support in Louth. Here we see the Louth Mission Brass Band. (Postcard.)

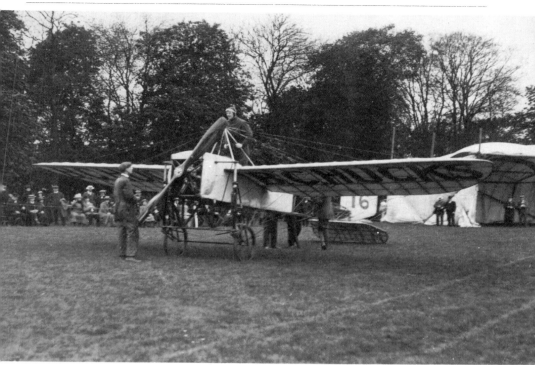

JUST BEFORE THE FIRST WORLD WAR, the aeroplane made its debut in Louth. This was B.C. Hucks and his 70 hp Bleriot monoplane. The photograph was taken on 13 June 1913 and Mr Hucks attracted large crowds, eager to see his fascinating form of travel; he usually gave demonstrations at the Cow Pastures. (Postcard c. 1913.)

HERE WE SEE THE OLD TEMPERANCE HOTEL on the left of Eastgate (the site is presently occupied by Grandways supermarket).

IN THIS VIEW of the Cornmarket Street's had the bow-fronted windows (fourth premises from the right) next to the Mason's Arms.

THIS WAS STREET'S THE CHEMIST in the Cornmarket selling an impressive array of cures and ointments. Mr Street later served on Louth Town Council and was one of the town's civic leaders.

WESTGATE, LOUTH.

IT WOULD BE VERY REMISS OF ME to complete a book on Louth without including a view of St James' Church from Westgate; it has been painted and photographed so often. This early postcard shows Westgate houses without the accoutrements they now possess.

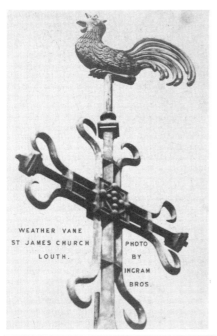

WEATHER VANE
ST JAMES CHURCH
LOUTH.
PHOTO
BY
INGRAM
BROS.

THE WEATHER VANE on the top of St James' Church was made from the great copper basin taken from the Scots at Flodden Field. It has been regilded a number of times including the occasion when this photograph was taken in 1915 when Arthur Ingram of Louth carried out the work. (Ingram Brothers.)

Watery Lane, Cawthorpe, near Louth

THIS TRANQUIL SCENE was to come to an end with the First World War. Before the motor car, people had relied heavily on the horse and cart. This photograph was taken at the Splash, Cawthorpe. (Postcard, Valentine Series.)

HERE WE SEE a group of Lincolnshire Yeomanry at the back of the Turk's Head. At the back (standing fourth from left, back row) is Mr Leslie who was the manager of the National Provincial (now National Westminster) in the Market Place. (J.S. Bullon of Grimsby and Louth.)

A FEW LUDENSIANS joined the Grimsby 'Chums'. Here we see their farewell visit on 19 May 1915. They made up the 10th Lincolns.

THEY HAD BEEN given ample training in Brocklesby Park, digging trenches and making ready for the 'war to end all wars'.

HAROLD LEONARD MATTHEWS (1892–1915) was killed in action on 13 October 1915. He was with the 5th Lincolns on that day when a section in Flanders known as the Hohenzollern Redoubt, claimed the lives of 12 officers and 285 other ranks. Harold Matthews was the eldest son of Joseph Matthews, photographer.

THE AFTERMATH OF THE FIRST WORLD WAR can be seen in these men's faces as they proudly march past in their spoon-polished boots and shoes. There is a certain air of despondency in their faces. (H.L. Howe.)

TAKING PART IN the parade on Mayors' Sunday, Louth, H.L. Howe captured three prominent businessmen. From left to right they were Mr Falkner, Mr Slater Eyre and Mr Larder. (H.L. Howe.)

A WAR MEMORIAL was erected in 1922. Designed by Harold Hall and built by Harrisons Stonemasons, it was placed at the junction of Eastgate with Ramsgate.

SECTION TWO

Between the Wars

BECAUSE LOUTH AND THE SURROUNDING AREA relied on animal husbandry, it was important that animals were well cared for. Vets have thrived in the town and F. Harlow's Medicine Store at No. 6 Queen Street was a by-product of that care. (H.L. Howe.)

IN THIS PHOTOGRAPH (the most recent in the book) we see the Princess Royal standing between Jim Laverack and Rosmary Lindop when she came to open the Louth Livestock Centre at the cattlemarket in January 1989. (*Louth Standard.*)

AFTER THE FIRST WORLD WAR soldiers returned to continue their lives where they had left off. This was the view of the market place. (Towle.)

WHILE THIS WAS the view of Eastgate. (Towle.)

IN THIS PHOTOGRAPH of St James' Church from the cattlemarket there is a flag flying on the top of the spire. This must have been quite a remarkable feat! Meanwhile there are old wooden fences which were used as pens (these were later replaced by metal ones) and the row of terraced cottages next to the Welcome Refreshment Rooms were often used by auctioneers for their Friday (cattlemarket day) dealings. (G.W. Dales.)

THE OLD PAPER-MILL viewed from Westgate fields was once a thriving business. As modern industrial methods replaced traditional ways of making paper the mill was forced to close. Then it became a flour-mill and latterly a trout farm before being converted into a housing development called Troutbeck.

ANOTHER VIEW OF THE MILL from the road shows some of the development that has taken place since its recent conversion into dwellings.

HUBBARDS HILLS WATER-MILL should not be confused with the old paper-mill which at one time belonged to Thorpe Hall. Hubbards Hills Water-Mill was always a flour-mill to complement the windmill which once stood just a few yards up the lane.

The Old Mill, Hubbards Valley, Louth.

IN THE LAST PHOTOGRAPH the chimney is clearly visible. In this snapshot taken in the 1920s the chimney has been knocked down. It was a picturesque spot, sadly neglected just recently, with sumptuous gardens and flowers of all descriptions.

JUST A SHORT DISTANCE AWAY FROM HUBBARDS HILLS WATER-MILL this Victorian pump-house was installed to provide the people of Louth with constant running water in their homes. There is still a waterworks on the same site today. Prior to this everyone had to draw their water from communal pumps or, for those who were fortunate enough to have pumps at the back of their houses, the maid had to go and pump every ounce that came into the household.

IF YOU LOOK CAREFULLY at this photograph of Hubbards Hills by A.E. Towle, the chimney is just visible appearing over the top of the bank.

THIS NEXT PHOTOGRAPH is Thorpe Hall again. One of the occupants of Thorpe Hall from 1938 to 1953 was Geoffrey Harmsworth, brother of Sir Harold Harmsworth – a member of that distinguished newspaper publishing family. When he sold Thorpe Hall to Sir John Marsden, he moved to Mrs Winteringham's White Cottage at Tealby. (Towle.)

MRS WINTERINGHAM, MP for Louth, came from the distinguished Grimbarian family of Abbey House (off Wellowgate) in Grimsby. She was the first English woman to be elected to parliament (the first woman MP was Mrs Astor – an American) showing that the suffragettes in Louth had much influence. When she moved from her cottage in Tealby she went to live in Minster Yard, Lincoln.

LOUTH EXPERIENCED the worst disaster it had known for 100 years on 29 May 1920 when the River Lud overflowed its banks and flooded the town. The area immediately around the Lud took the brunt of the damage. This was Enginegate at the bottom of Broadbank.

LOUTH DISASTER, 29/5/20   No. 42 BEHIND ENGINEGATE

ANOTHER VIEW OF ENGINEGATE — this time by W. Benton, photographer of No. 82 Rye Hill, Newcastle-upon-Tyne.

IN THIS REMARKABLE photograph of the junction of Ramsgate with Commercial Road, we see a man up a lamp-post, while other onlookers view the flood from their bedroom windows.

DURING THE FLOOD yet another remarkable photograph was taken of a group of men lashed together with a length of rope while wading through the water to reach the houses in the distance. It was feared that the terrace might collapse at any time as this heroic band made its rescue bid.

he Louth Disaster. May 29rh 1920.

W. Benton
82 RyaHill

CLEANING UP THE MESS after the flood was a laborious operation. An evil smelling silt covered everything and household belongings had to be rescued. This photograph of an area just off Eve Street in 1920 is a particularly good example of the damage that was caused to ordinary people's homes. (W. Benton.)

YET ANOTHER BENTON VIEW showing the aftermath of the flood with hapless victims drying out their precious possessions – in this case a piano,

THIS IS ONE OF A SET OF POSTCARDS produced by the now defunct *Yorkshire Observer*.

THERE ARE ENOUGH PHOTOGRAPHS of the Louth flood to fill a book. The reason for this profusion was a local by-election which attracted photographers and media men alike. This picture shows Tuxworth's, now McCleod's store in Bridge Street. The people in the picture, taken in 1920, were (from left to right): Nell Tuxworth, Mrs Cottam, Mrs Tuxworth senior, Chris Tuxworth, Ernest Sowerby and two workmen.

IN THE AFTERMATH OF THE FLOOD fish was brought from Grimsby to dole out to the needy victims.

AT THE JUNCTION OF NICHOL HILL with Little Eastgate stands this fine old house. Originally built as a town house, it has since been divided into two separate dwellings.

PLATTS GROCERY STORE (second from left) was next to the Wesleyan Chapel with Sharpley's the solicitors in the building at the end before the impressive frontage of Louth Town Hall.

MANY PEOPLE WILL REMEMBER BILLY PLATT'S STORE in Little Eastgate on the site of the present Parkers bookshop. Here we see Billy Platt's father standing outside his provisions shop (c. 1920). The shop which was started by Billy Platt's great-uncle, Mr Howsam, traded for 102 years until it closed in 1985.

CHARABANC PARTIES were popular during the twenties. It was a quicker mode of travel than the old horse and cart. This photograph was probably taken at the back of the White Hart (now demolished) in Aswell Street, c. 1925. (H.L. Howe.)

YET ANOTHER CHARABANC PARTY. This time outside the Wheatsheaf Inn in Westgate.

CARLTON CRICKET CLUB (C. 1924). The front row were (from left to right): Cook (a schoolmaster at Grimoldby), Bosworth (umpire), Revd Loft (vicar of Great and Little Carlton's churches), Walt Holroyd, Will Versey (a joiner in Little Carlton), Will Holroyd and Clarke. On the back row extreme left is Merrikin and fourth from left is Jack Speed (a pig slaughterer).

ON THE LOUTH GIRLS' GRAMMAR SCHOOL PLAYING FIELDS between the Horncastle Road and Julian Bower, three young tennis hopefuls pose for a photograph, C. 1925. They were (from left to right): Mary Hall, Vera Ellis (sitting down) and Cathy Warne. Both rackets and dress are evocative of the twenties.

WHEN PRIME MINISTER STANLEY BALDWIN visited Louth on 21 July 1927, Major Vigor-Fox and Colonel Heneage MP were there to meet him at Louth Station. Baldwin's visit was brief as he was whisked away to give a speech at Hainton Hall. All the boys of Westgate School lined up to watch him pass. Stanley Baldwin (second from right) is seen here with Mrs Baldwin in the centre.

THERE WAS A TIME when blacksmiths, wheelwrights and agricultural engineers abounded in Louth. One of the last to survive was Howard's on Upgate. It was situated next to the cattlemarket and so within easy reach of farmers when they came into town to conduct their business. Here we see George Howard c. 1927 in front of his workshop.

HUBBARDS HILLS are a favourite spot with many neighbouring towns and villages. Here we see the Grimsby LNER Musical Society's picnic which took place in the Hills in 1928. (H.L. Howe.)

BEFORE THE LOUTH PLAYGOERS CAME INTO BEING, there were other groups who put on plays and entertainment in Louth. This one, entitled *The Upper Room*, was a passion play produced at Louth Town Hall by St Michael's Church Amateur Dramatic Society. Achaz (played by Reg Smith – seated on the right) was the landlord of the inn in which there was an upper room. The scene throughout was set for the Last Supper and the play ran each evening to 'free' houses. (H.L. Howe.)

BEFORE THE LOUTH PLAYGOERS MOVED INTO THE THEATRE on Newmarket, it was the Wesleyan Sunday School. Here we see a Christmas get-together with presents, prizes and decorations. (H.L. Howe.)

TWO GREAT CHARACTER ACTORS from the early days of Louth Playgoers were Percy Wilson (left) and Reg Cash. This scene is from the Playgoers production of *Saloon Bar* in 1949.

BEFORE THE FORMATION of Louth Amateur Operatic Society, there were many concert parties, of which this was one.

LOUTH AMATEUR OPERATIC SOCIETY'S production of *The Desert Song* in 1935 featured one of Louth's great heart-throbs of the thirties. John Harrison who played The Red Shadow – a sort of a latter day Rudolph Valentino – captured the hearts of many Louth audiences.

HERE HARRISON is dressed as The Red Shadow.

MARGARET GODSMARK played opposite Harrison.

... AND MR ROBINSON, the greengrocer, was one of the supporting cast.

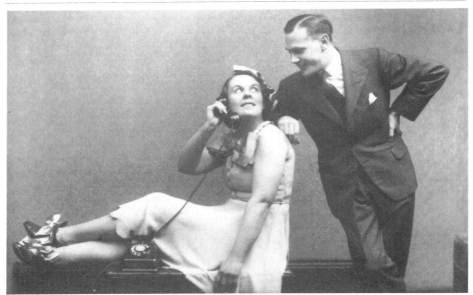

ANOTHER POPULAR COUPLE from those days in the Louth Operatic Society's productions was Joyce Parker (left) and Jimmy Wilson. This is from the 1939 production of *The Girlfriend*. Joyce Parker was to join ENSA in the war.

THE LOUTH PLAYGOERS production of *Rookery Nook* by Ben Travers in 1934. Gerald Popkiss (extreme left) has his hand on Harold Twine's shoulder and is saying 'Harold's just told a beauty!' Gerald was played by C.S. Rowland and Harold by R. Wardlow Clokie.

DURING THE THIRTIES AND FORTIES Louth Playgoers staged many fine performances in the local cinema. As their confidence grew and their popularity increased they decided to build a new theatre. This was some of the cast from their first ever production in the Newmarket Theatre. The play was *Square Pegs* and the cast included (from left to right): Hugh Neale, Irene Godsmark, Margaret Wright, Dorothy Wilson, Brenda Fytche and Nick Allery.

THE LOUTH PLAYGOERS could draw talent from the hopeful budding actors and actresses of the Grammar School. Here we see the cast from *Henry IV* (part I) staged in the Grammar School c. 1941. (H.L. Howe.)

CRAFTSMEN ABOUNDED in Louth at the turn of the century. This was Herbert Tyson of Newmarket who was responsible for making many stringed instruments. He also encouraged many youngsters in their appreciation of music. Here we see him at his bench putting the finishing touches to a viola. (H.L. Howe.)

PUTTING SOME OF TYSON'S INSTRUMENTS to good use are a group of children from Kidgate School. Brian Howe is on the extreme left while the late Peter Smith, butcher of Upgate and future Mayor of Louth, is fourth from the left.

THE BRITISH SCHOOL is just visible at the top of Kidgate. Although it is fashionable to look back with nostalgia life was not a bed of roses for everyone; you can almost smell the poverty oozing out of this scene. c. 1919–20. (H.L. Howe.)

SEATED IN THE CENTRE OF THIS GROUP was Humphrey Phillipps Walcot-Burton, vicar of St James from 1928–1951. He came to Louth from Crosby, Scunthorpe, when he succeeded Canon Lenton. Many of Louth's prominent 'citizens' gathered for this group shot including Dr Laughton-Smith (to Burton's left) and just behind him is Owen Price (bespectacled) who was the organist at St James from 1897 to 1946. On Laughton-Smith's left is the familiar figure of Percy Latter (headmaster of Kidgate School). (H.L. Howe.)

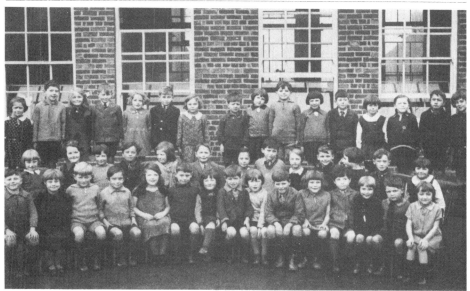

IN THE THIRTIES the British School was known as Kidgate School. It had been enlarged and was capable of taking more pupils.

CRICKET HAS ALWAYS BEEN POPULAR in Louth ever since Louth & District Cricket Club was formed in 1822. Here we see a game in the thirties when the old stand was in use. This stand (roughly sited where the sports hall stands today) was dismantled and moved to the Horncastle Road ground. (H.L. Howe.)

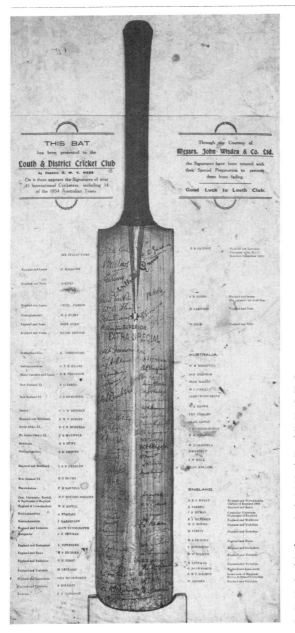

ONE OF THE MOST REMARKABLE PRESENTATIONS made to Louth Cricket Club was this piece of cricket memorabilia. The bat was presented in 1934 by Captain G.W.V. Webb with a note from Wisdens saying that signatures had been treated with a varnish to stop them from fading. It also wished 'Good Luck to Louth Club' and among the 45 signatures of international cricketers (which included 14 of the 1934 Australian Test Team) were: Jack Hobbs, Harold Larwood, Voce, Sutcliffe, Leyland, Wyatt, Bowes, Verity, Rhodes and Nichols. From the Australian team the names included: Wordfull, Don Bradman, Stan McCabe, Les Darling, Ponsford and Hans Ebeling.

TYPICAL OF THE MANY FANCY DRESS PARTIES in the thirties was this one of 1930 held in the old Liberal Club in Queen Street. The costumes were as imaginative as they were varied.

YET ANOTHER LIBERAL CLUB CHILDREN'S FANCY DRESS PARTY. This one took place on 19 January 1934. In the centre of this group (second row from the back, eighth from the left) is Basil Lock. He is the smiling boy with a crown on his head, later to become a distinguished Air Vice-Marshal who, among other things, taught the Duke of Edinburgh to fly an aeroplane. (H.L. Howe.)

TYPICAL OF THE DANCES HELD IN THE TOWN HALL during the twenties and thirties was this Conservative Ball. Set in the early thirties there is a small banner with a song of that period *You can't play my Ukulele!* heralding the popularity of George Formby. Towards the end of the twenties flounced dresses of lace ciré proved to be fashionable with their uneven hem-lines while men still wore stiff starched collars.

'HELLO, HELLO, HELLO, WHAT'S ALL THIS THEN?' This group of men might appear to be competing for the part of Inspector Poirot but in fact it is a police dinner held in the thirties in the Town Hall. They were (from left to right, back row): Mr Cullington, Supt. Dunham, Inspector Dodson, Tasker, Goodwin and Inspector Killick; (front row) Mrs Cullington, Mrs Dunham, Mrs Dodson, Mrs Tasker and Mrs Killick. (H.L. Howe.)

EVERY YEAR THERE WAS A FOOTBALL MATCH to raise money for Crowtree Lane Hospital (these were the days before the NHS). The match was always played on the London Road sports ground and here we see the cup being presented to a victorious team in the twenties. What is noticeable is the man to the right of the photograph who only has one leg and a crutch. First World War veterans and other injured persons had seats reserved for them in front of the stand.

AFTER THE ABDICATION OF EDWARD VIII in 1936, George VI came to the throne. This was the coronation tea party held at Monk's Dyke School where special coronation mugs were presented to the children. Donald Pleasence, the actor, is probably the most famous old boy of this school. (H.L. Howe.)

A GROUP OF LOUTH GRAMMAR SCHOOL BOYS about to take part in a steeple chase. The year is 1933 and the boy (fourth from the right) on the back row is Jenkinson who later managed the Mason's Arms pub in the Cornmarket for many years. (H.L. Howe.)

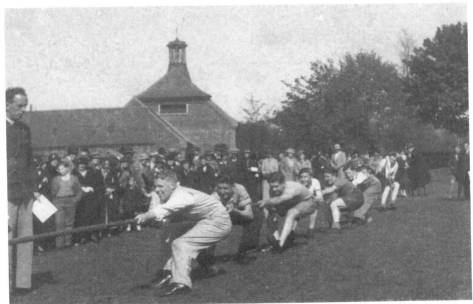

A TUG OF WAR on the Grammar School playing fields in the thirties.

LOUTH GRAMMAR SCHOOL FOOTBALL TEAM of 1932–3. From left to right the back row were: H. Hauton, A. Hopcroft, S. Winn, C. Dolling, R. Ilett, J.H. Walker. Front row: R. Forman, J. Perkins, M. Hibbitt (capt.) C. Freshney and F. Masters. The photograph was taken by Clare photographers of Louth.

ONE OF THE MOST POPULAR RESTAURANTS in Louth in the thirties was Hansons in Upgate. Here we see it decorated for the 1936 Agricultural show. (H.L. Howe.)

HANSON'S ALSO DID OUTSIDE CATERING. In this photograph we see the staff dressed in white hats and pinafores at the Town Hall. Mrs Hanson is standing in the back row (third from the right) with Mr Heward on her right. (H.L. Howe.)

THE SPIRE OF ST JAMES CHURCH was in sore need of restoration in the thirties. The whole of this work was carried out for a mere £5,000. I hate to think how much it would cost today. (H.L. Howe.)

ONE FINE DAY in the summer of 1934, a group of Pony Club enthusiasts rode over to the New Inn at Saltfleet. The group consisted of Maple Bedford, Miss Wyer Honey, Bridget Gardener, Marie Crow, Lauraine, Miss Elvin, Ena and Kee. After their picnic they returned to Louth.

OVER THE YEARS the Maiden Row Baths did some sterling service. Originally opened in 1924, they lasted for 50 years until the new Louth swimming pool was built in 1974 on the corner of Victoria Road with Ramsgate. (H.L. Howe.)

THE MAIDEN ROW BATHS were still going strong in the 1960s, but it was felt that Louth needed a new swimming pool. Here we see a young Katherine Czornyj (now Robinson) aged 12 sitting in a bath as part of the carnival parade float to raise money and public awareness that 'Louth needs a Bigger BATH'! The photograph was taken at the cattlemarket in 1962.

LOOKING UP CHURCH STREET, Louth Baths were on the right-hand side of the road after the buildings where Allinson & Wilcox printers are now situated. Meanwhile the buildings in the immediate foreground have all been demolished to make way for the bus station.

ON THE OTHER SIDE of Church Street this block of Georgian terraces was demolished in the sixties to make way for Elizabeth Court old people's home.

BEFORE THE BUS STATION moved to its present site on the corner of Queen Street and Church Street, it was situated in the Market Place. (H.L. Howe.)

THE ONCE FAMILIAR sight of the Cleethorpes to King's Cross train going through Louth is one that we shall see no more. The track was taken up after Beeching's famous cut when Louth Station fell victim to a piece of short-sighted governmental policy in 1935. (H.L. Howe.)

LOUTH HAS BEEN HOME to numerous religious denominations. Here we see the old Primitive Methodist Chapel in Northgate which was used as Pickfords' warehouse. It was demolished in the mid-seventies when the roof caved in. (Edward Lund.)

IN THE EARLY DAYS of the Second World War, Churchill visited Louth. At that time Park House (now the Lincolnshire Poacher pub) in Eastgate was the HQ for the Coldstreams, Grenadiers and Hampshires. It was here that Churchill stopped overnight. However, in this photograph we see the old Duke of Gloucester (third from left) chatting to one or two men in Lacey Gardens.

SHORTLY BEFORE THE outbreak of the Second World War, this was the Remembrance Service held in front of the War Memorial at the corner of Eastgate with Ramsgate in 1938. (H.L. Howe.)

DURING ONE OF those lighter moments in the Second World War, a group of people had time to pose for a photograph on the ever popular stepping stones on Hubbards Hills. They were (from left to right) the manager of Boots, a small girl, Viv Griffiths, Wynn Peal, Mrs Vinter, D. Lee and Jack.

DURING THE WAR YEARS, Louth organized its own special concert party. They entertained the public, troops and the RAF, often visiting farms, small village halls and aerodromes under blackout restrictions. This meant their driver had to have a keen pair of eyes and quick reactions as they travelled along roads with dimmed lights or sometimes no lights at all. The concert party comprises (from left to right) Hugh Efemey (tenor), Daisy Lee (singer), Sydney Platt (pianist), Reg Cash (comedian), Cyril Holland (the butt of most of the fun and nicknamed 'our Enoch'), Reg Smith (comedian and violinist), Sydney Smith (baritone), Jessie Ainger (singer) and B. Carter Eastwood (who sang and played the ukulele).

JOHN ROBERT SANDERSON was Mayor of Louth in 1944. The group (from left to right) were: Mr Heward (mace-bearer), Jack Sanderson, Mrs Sanderson and the Town Clerk.

LOUTH WAS BOMBED sporadically in the Second World War. One of the unfortunate families to receive a direct hit was the Jaines family who lived on the Grimsby Road. Here we see in happier times (from left to right): Marjory Brown, (secretary of the firm), Mrs Jaines, Arthur Jaines (holding young Michael Jaines), Len Jaines and Mrs Betty Jaines (holding young John Jaines later a noted athlete).

After the Second World War and the Fifties

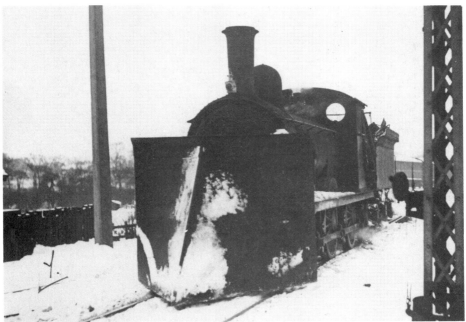

IN THAT MISERABLE winter of 1947 Louth was cut off completely and it was necessary to bring out the snow-ploughs. (H.L. Howe.)

WHEN MR JAINES first started his haulage firm it is unlikely that he could have perceived the damage that lorries would do to Louth in the latter part of this century.

THE JAINES FLEET of lorries had grown out of all proportion by 1949. This photograph was taken on the old RAF field at Manby.

THE MAYORAL PROCESSION through Louth of 1947 when Wilfred Slack was Mayor. Here we see an ageing Vigor-Fox (the gentleman in the pin-stripe suit holding a mackintosh over one arm). Sir John Vigor-Fox was High Sheriff of Lincolnshire in 1906 and was knighted in 1939. He was High Steward of Louth for many years until his resignation in 1960. He died at Pilton, Somerset in 1968.

AFTER THE WAR people returned to their jobs and soldiers went back to civvy street. This view on Mr Brown's farm at Burwell gives a hint of the machinery to come. There were great strides in automation during the war. Locals said 'Them combine harvester's 'll not replace stowking' but they did. The machine in this photograph is a reaper-binder.

THIS AERIAL VIEW of Ramsgate overlooking Alexandra Road, Eastgate and Monks Dyke Road was taken from the Malt Kiln (c. 1950) by Les Howe. It shows how much development has taken place in recent years. The hut in the foreground is now a block of flats, the East Lincs Motor Company building is currently a supermarket and there has been a plethora of new houses erected mostly on allotments or wasteground.

ANOTHER CASUALTY of the war years was the Malt Kiln which was bombed. When the new kiln was erected and completed in 1951 it was the largest malt silo in Europe. it is still a blot on the landscape. (H.L. Howe.)

ONE OF THE MOST interesting photographs taken from the top of the Malt Kiln was this one showing Holy Trinity Church to the left of the picture. This entire area is now a mass of housing development.

MERCER ROW IN the 1950s shows that certain storekeepers such as Day Bros. were still allowed to display their wares in the street. The cars of that era are now collector's items. (Valentine postcard.)

AT THIS DINNER in the old Drill Hall in Victoria Road (now the Library headquarters) we see a group of ex-servicemen including on the left Capt. Benton and Mrs Benton and on the right Mrs Howe, Major Howe, Capt. Lee and Mrs Lee at a Territorial reunion in the 1950s.

AFTER THE WAR, Great Britain had been drained of financial resources. There was much encouragement to save hence National Savings. Here we see a rally held in Lincoln during April 1955 to commemorate the constituencies represented. Cecil Simpson is holding the Louth banner. (*North Lincolnshire and Louth Advertiser.*)

A FATHER AND SON join the Territorials in the early sixties. From left to right the group includes Major Clive Bacon, Sgt. Lambley, John Lill and Wilfred and John Maltby. (Bert Rawlings.)

IN THE FIFTIES Louth Station was still going strong. Here we see some of the staff with a particularly fine dray horse to pull the delivery cart. (H.L. Howe.)

THIS IS A photograph of the first diesel engine to work in Louth Station. It was mostly used to shunt carriages and wagons from one track to the other. (S. Lee.)

THE OTHER MODE of transport was the bus. Buses left Louth regularly for Grimsby, going through a myriad of small villages including Fotherley, Utterby and Ludborough before taking a breather at North Thoresby. (*North Lincolnshire and Louth Advertiser.*)

THIS IS A GROUP of schoolchildren from North Thorseby. The photograph is dated December 1955 and shows the styles of children's clothes in that post war period.

SHORTLY BEFORE THE demise of the *North Lincolnshire and Louth Advertiser*, some of the staff met in Hanson's café. Louth has been fortunate to possess two local papers for the last 150 years. In the fifties the other paper was the *Louth Standard*. In this photograph in the 1950s it is possible to recognize Arthur Milnes (standing extreme left), the small smiling stature of 'Woggy' Ashton (front row; fifth from the left), Tom Boyden (extreme right), Bert Hallam (back row ninth from the left) and Cecil Simpson (fourth from left).

MAURICE HALL WAS Mayor of Louth in 1950. He is seen here at the County Hospital Ball (second from the left). Hall's musical shop in Eastgate brought the twentieth century to Louth. In the fifties, when pop records made their debut, he had to adjust to cope with demand.

LUDAMEATIES MOVED to Thames Street on the site of the old gasworks in 1962. Here we see two of the silos being built. Now part of BP Nutrition, it is one of the biggest dog biscuit factories in England.

LUDAMEATIES DOG BISCUIT FACTORY in Eve Street suffered a huge fire on 23 April 1952 which gutted the premises. Ludameaties, one of Louth's most successful firms, was started back in 1938 by Freeman, a butcher in New Street and Sutcliffe. Within a short time Sutcliffe had pulled out and Elliott 'Jack' Brook realized the potential of this small individual firm. (*North Lincolnshire and Louth Advertiser.*)

UTTERBY'S ANSWER TO the ever popular *Brains Trust* programme was to produce their own team. On 15 March 1952 Utterby Toc H gathered together a team. They were (from left to right): Revd Holt, Commander Fenton-Thiede, Major Streather, Mr Street (the compare), Mr H. Dyer (headmaster of Alford Grammar School), Mr J. Neal, P. Cordeaux and Mr C. Neal. It was all great fun.

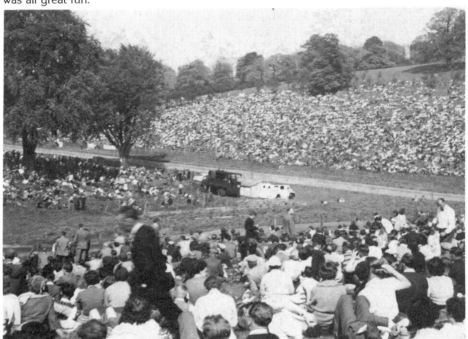

ONE OF THE GREAT attractions near Louth is Cadwell Park. Known throughout Europe as a racing circuit, it has attracted all the best motor-cycle aces including Barry Sheene, Agostinni and Wayne Gardner. Although it was only started in this century when local heroes such as Beeton and Frith were tearing around the track it has come a long way since then. This photograph was taken in the fifties and it is possible to see the circuit's popularity from the mass of people.

ONE OF THE FEW REMAINING WORKING WATER-MILLS in the country is this one at Alvingham. Carefully renovated by Mr and Mrs Davies it is the only working water-mill in the district. In its heyday the River Lud powered thirteen water-mills – only Alvingham now remains. The Bett family owned it for nearly a hundred years, William Bett bought it at auction in the Fleece in 1866 and his son Tom Bett continued to use it as a mill when this photograph was taken in 1953. (*North Lincolnshire and Louth Advertiser.*)

H.L. HOWE (1897–1959) with camera and tripod looking up at the spire of St James' Church from Chequergate (c. 1953). This was a case of a photographer taking a photograph of a photographer taking a photograph.

LACEY GARDENS INFANT OR JUNIOR SCHOOL (c. 1953) when the teacher was Mrs Wyers. Occasionally the local press run a 'Where are they now?' feature – this group could prove to be interesting.

THIS WAS A VIEW of the coal yard next to the station. It is an evocative photograph with a Pickford's van and a lone cart in the foreground. (S. Lee.)

LOOKING DOWN EASTGATE we can see that the business names have changed but the buildings look remarkably similar to today. I suspect this photograph was taken on a Sunday since it is unusually quiet. (H.L. Howe.)

OVER THE YEARS Louth Playgoers have put on some surprising performances. Many students have been put through their paces on the Louth stage including Lewis Collins (Bodie), Patricia Hodge and Prunella Gee when they were students with LAMDA. This was the cast of the 1952 production of *Worm's Eye View* when the cast included: Hugh Neale, John Lill, Arthur Miles, Leslie Saweard (now Christine of *The Archers*), Gilbert Pitt, Lilian Gray, Bill Summers, Jack Marks and Gron Parry. The front row comprised: Reg Cash, Poppy Graves and Jack Bennett. (Bert Rawlings.)

THIS WAS THE LOUTH PLAYGOERS' PRODUCTION of *The Hasty Heart* produced in February 1953. From left to right the cast included: Brenda Fytche, John Wilcox, John Parrish, Arthur Miles, Norman Ashworth, Jack Bennett (who took the part played by Richard Todd in the film), Nick Allery and John Lill (who played the part taken by Ronald Reagan in the film). (Bert Rawlings.)

WHEN THE ROCK 'N ROLL era hit Louth, it replaced the old time dances at the Liberal Club. This photograph taken in the Northgate Baptists Chapel shows some early exponants of the dance typifying those who danced in the aisles of the Playhouse cinema when *Rock Around the Clock* was first shown in Louth. (H.L. Howe.)

IN A LIGHTER VEIN this was the pancake race held in North Somercotes in 1953.

WHEN LOUTH LIBRARY OPENED in Upgate in 1953, Frank MacDonald was Mayor. He is seen here at the opening on the extreme left. The library replaced the old Mechanics Institute in Upgate and remains there today. It was officially opened by Lieut. Col. Sir Weston Cracroft Amcotts. (*North Lincolnshire and Louth Advertiser.*)

THERE WAS MUCH INVESTMENT during the fifties in new roads. At Swaby it was felt that the road needed widening to cope with increased traffic. The year is 1952.

BURNING THOSE DREADFUL ration books in 1953 on the fire in the Louth Conservative offices (now the *Louth Standard* building).

LOOKING DOWN ASWELL STREET there have been a number of changes. All of the houses on the left of this photograph have been demolished to make way for shops. Interestingly, one of these buildings was a doll's hospital.

ON THE OTHER side of Aswell Street old buildings were knocked down to make way for Kirby's Electrical Showroom. We may view this as cheap and nasty now but at one time this was modernization.

AT THE JUNCTION of Kidgate with Upgate, Mawer Brothers had a ramshackle showroom advertising their funereal stone masonry. The site is where Alfred's restaurant is currently situated. (Edward Land.)

AT THE BACK of the King's Head, this archway led through to some stables at the rear of this old hotel. (Eward Land.)

THE BRITISH LEGION band in the fifties. Photographed in Eastgate by H.L. Howe.

JOSEPH BENNETT OF DEIGHTON CLOSE lived to be 100. This was 'young Joe' as opposed to 'old Joe' (his father). Joseph Bennett was born in 1854 the son of Joseph Bennett, former MP for Gainsborough. 'Young Joe' would frequently travel to the family timber business in Victoria Street, Grimsby, by train even when he was 80 years old!

INSIDE DEIGHTON CLOSE (1950), the heavily decorated Edwardian drawing-room was sumptuous by any standards. Deighton Close is now a residential school for maladjusted boys.

LOUTH RIFLE CLUB originated from the old Louth Volunteers. Here we see a group of them in the early fifties with a clutch of trophies; they are (from left to right): Bill Paulson, Ron Laking, Major Boswell, Alderman Maxey, Ron Mawer, Bill Platt and Bill Richardson. (Bert Rawlings.)

WILLIAM ROBERT BURR was Mayor of Louth in 1954 (centre of picture). Here we see him at a dinner with this group who were (from left to right): Cyril Osborne MP, Mrs Maxey, Mrs Burr, Mr Burr, Mrs Gaskin (formerly Miss Batchelor of Batchelor Foods), Eric West and Mrs Osborne.

THIS WAS LOUTH TRADE FAIR which was held in the Town Hall in 1954. Demonstrating some of the kitchen appliances is T. Topley, while Jill Osborne (daughter of the MP) tries one out. The people in the photograph are (from left to right): Cyril Osborne MP, Chris Sandwith, Jill Osborne, T. Topley, Mrs Burr and William Burr (the Mayor).

NEW SHOP WINDOWS were installed at the back of Eve & Ranshaw's store in 1954 ambiguously sporting the initials of E.R. in the centre top panes. (The coronation of Elizabeth II had only taken place the year before.) This part of Eve & Ranshaw's premises is currently Mr Martin's hairdressing salon and Precedence Men's Wear.

THIS GROUP OF PEOPLE was present at the opening of the Lincolnshire Poacher in Eastgate on 7 August 1954. From left to right they were: John Barber (the Borough Surveyor), Mrs Ellis, Mr Ellis (of the firm Ellis, Thompson & Co.) and Councillor B. Gibson. Flowers Breweries converted the old Park House, once the Headquarters of Eastern Command, into what promised to be Louth's newest hotel.

AT THE WORKING MEN'S CLUB Christmas Draw in December 1955 we see a festive array of turkeys and Scotch. The group in the top photograph are (from left to right): Harold 'Lofty' Allen, –?–, Mr Dannatt, Starsmore, Bill Dann, 'Sparks' Clarke, Harry Kime, Mr Dann and Bill Scott. In the photographs below Mr Dann announces some of the lucky prizewinners. (*North Lincolnshire and Louth Advertiser.*)

Bottom, right.
THE LOUTH CHRYSANTHEMUM FAYRE was usually held in October to raise money for the church. In the fifties St James' needed £50,000 for urgent restoration. An appeal was set up and you can just see a thermometer showing the various amounts of monies raised, in the right-hand corner of this picture. Lady Yarborough opened the 1955 fayre and this was the bottle stall. The three ladies immediately behind the stall are, from left to right, J. Nielson, Maple Bedford and Ann Nickerson while the lady, second from the right, is Miss Falkner (later to become Mrs Sharpley).

A GROUP OF LOUTH GIRL GUIDES in July 1955. Standing on the back row (third from left) is Miss Cordeaux MBE who lived in the large Victorian mansion at Cordeaux Corner. She was one of the stalwarts of Louth Red Cross and the name has been retained in Cordeaux High School on High Holme Road.

LINCOLNSHIRE IS MADE up of characters – this was Mrs Jacklin of Saltfleet photographed when she was 99 in 1955.

ANOTHER LOCAL CHARACTER captured at the Mablethorpe Carnival of 1955 was Commander Maitland MP of Harrington Hall. In the centre of the picture complete with stick, hand in pocket and hat he was a familiar figure in and around Louth. The photograph is by F.J. Soar of Victoria Road, Mablethorpe.

THE GRAMMAR SCHOOL has always enjoyed a high academic standard, fostering a host of bright young men. This was their prizegiving in 1955.

ALTHOUGH THIS PHOTOGRAPH of Wilfred Pickles and Mabel was taken in Mablethorpe, after the disastrous floods of 1953, when his famous radio programme *Have a Go* visited the coastal resort, Wilfred Pickles also came to Louth. The year was 1955 and many people can remember queuing to catch a glimpse of this well-known radio personality.

AT A HARVEST SALE on behalf of Louth Methodist Church, Mr Stevenson (the auctioneer) presided over the bidding. To his right (the man with his hand on his hip) is John Starsmore, Mayor of Louth in 1952 and 1959, while others in the group included Mr Growcott, Shucksmith, Addison, Robertson, Borrill and Mr A.E. Hand. The sale took place on 5 November at the Central Hall, Nichol Hill.

THERE WAS A PONY CLUB CAMP at Welton-le-Wold in 1955 which lasted for about a week. It involved three hunts, including the Southwold Hunt and over a hundred people attended. In this group shot we see (from left to right) on the back row: –?–, Barbara Burt, Ann Sutton-Nelthorpe, Col. Guy Cubbitt, Donald Burt (Master of Foxhounds) and David Spencer. Front row (from left to right): Mrs Montieff, Miss Elvin, Mrs Popoff, Miss Wyer Honey, Maple Marfleet, a pony club instructor, Winnie Trafford, Mrs Jessop and 'Babe' English.

THESE WERE some of the younger set to attend that same Pony Club camp. On the back row third from the left is a young Mrs Ranby of Grimblethorpe Hall. (*North Lincolnshire and Louth Advertiser.*)

LOUTH FOOTBALL TEAM in 1954 when the goalkeeper was Fred Bourne.

LOUTH CRICKET TEAM (c. 1955) consisted of (back row from left to right): Dick Butler, Mick Lee, Burt Bosworth, Harry Younger, a serviceman from Manby, Van Cuylenburg and Arthur Miles (the umpire). Front row, from left to right: Ernie Bosworth, George Charlton, John Chapman, Maurice Hibbitt and Freddie Bourne.

H.L. HOWE USED to enjoy watching cricket. Here is a shot of Alan Stubbs hooking a ball to the boundary. Stubbs played for Louth Cricket Club although he lived in Saltfleetby.

ANOTHER BELLIGERENT BATSMAN was R.E. (Ted) Cook who played for Louth. Cook lived in Grainthorpe.

THIS WAS A CRICKET CLUB DINNER in the fifties and the people in the picture were, from right to left: Barry Mountain, Joan Smith, Bernard Smith and Ernie Bosworth.

IN THE FIFTIES it was necessary to introduce a Ministry of Food Welfare Scheme whereby the poor of the community could benefit. It was particularly aimed at mothers with young children. This photograph was taken in Louth in November 1955. Mrs Dunham is in the centre (back row) while Peggy Burton is on the extreme right.

ST JOHN'S AMBULANCE march past the Town Hall led by Charlie Cummings in 1955.

ST JAMES' CHURCH, LOUTH has always needed money prompting many ingenious schemes to provide for it. Here we see a craft stall selling all manner of home-made wares to raise cash for the church. Mr Chappell is second from the left and Mrs Godfrey is fourth from the left with Jim Lusby standing behind her. Mrs Hanson is fifth from the right and Canon Ward on the extreme right. This stall made up part of the Church Bazaar held in the Town Hall in 1955.

A CHEQUE for £1,760 made up from the monies received from the craft stall was handed over to Canon Ward. The people in this photograph are, from left to right: Phyllis West, Canon Ward, Mr Nelson, Mrs Sawyer, Mrs Thomson (Dr Thomson's wife) and Mrs Nielsen.

LOUTH HAS ALWAYS BEEN WELL SUPPLIED WITH FRESH FISH from Grimsby. Here we see a tramp supper in 1955 when the main course consisted of fish 'n chips wrapped in greaseproof paper.

THIS WAS THE MEET in the Cornmarket.

THE BOXING DAY MEET of the Southwold Hunt still takes place at the cattlemarket.

149

AFTER RETAINING HIS SEAT in the General Election of 1955 here we see the victorious Cyril Osborne in Louth. He beat the Labour candidate Dr Poirrer from Winterton near Scunthorpe into second place. Holding his arm is his wife (with a bunch of flowers in her other arm) and on the other side is his daughter.

THE FOLLOWING YEAR, 1955, Mr Maxey was Mayor of Louth yet again. Seen here with an officer from Manby it is interesting to note that the Royal Air Force College of Air Warfare was awarded the Honorary Freedom of Louth in 1965.

ALBERT ERNEST MAXEY was Louth's most frequent mayor. During his term of office in 1955–6 one of his duties was to present a Gold Badge to Reg Smith for his British Legion work. At the British Legion presentation on 3 March 1956 we see, left to right: Mr Haxby (the farmer), A.E. Maxey (Mayor), Reg B. Smith, Mr George Baggaley and R.H. Brunt. (*North Lincolnshire and Louth Advertiser*.)

ANOTHER PRESENTATION WAS of this clock to the retiring secretary of the Cannon Street Club, Mr Howard. The people in this photograph were, from left to right: Jack Richardson, Maxey, Mr Bott, Mr Howard and H.O. Smith.

ONE OF MRS MAXEY'S duties as Lady Mayoress during 1955 was to make this Red Cross presentation. The month was December and from the people in this group it is possible to distinguish: Mrs Harrison and Mrs Hobden on the extreme left, Mrs Maxey in the centre and Miss Cordeaux on the extreme right (standing behind the young girl). The gentleman in the middle with the moustache and glasses is Herbert Gregory. The photograph was by Bert Rawlings.

A LOUTH ANTS. & NATS. presentation to Mr Robinson, the fruiterer and nurseryman. Also in the picture (from left to right) are: Mr White, Miss Powell, Mr L. Ottaway, Mr Robinson (senior), Jack Yates presenting the plate-clock, Mr Robinson (junior), 'Toddy' Hall and Cecil Simpson, (c. 1955).

THE FIRST ANNUAL BALL of the Grenadier Guards Association was held in Louth on 25 February 1955. It ran successfully for many years. Tickets for the dinner-dance cost 15s. Here we see a group in Louth Town Hall; from left to right they are: Tony Cole, Mrs Crow, George Ash, Mrs Ash, Mrs Cooper, Steve Lee, Mrs Lee, –?–, Bill Horne, 'Jimmy' Cooper, Brian Emery, Joe Rodgers, –?– and 'Spud' Murphy.

TO MARK THE EVENT in 1955 there was a march past in Eastgate with the band of the Grenadiers blazing away. Mr Maxey, the Mayor, looked on with the Town Clerk on his left and Capt. Steve Lee on his right while this impressive spectacle paraded before him. It must have been a memorable occasion with the Grenadiers dressed in full uniform, including bearskins marching through the streets of Louth.

THAT CHRISTMAS OF 1955, there was a march past of a different sort. These were the nurses of Crowtree Lane Hospital singing carols for the patients. The nurse on the extreme left of the picture (with spectacles) was Sister Lily Doe. (Bert Rawlings.)

A LORRY TESTING THE GRADIENT of Aswell Street under snow (February 1956).

AN OLD PEOPLE'S tea party at Mount Pleasant, Louth in 1956 when Neil Ashley (the accordian player) put on the entertainment. Miss Proctor – now Mrs Davy (the young girl seated on the extreme right of the photograph) obviously enjoyed the music too. (*North Lincolnshire and Louth Advertiser.*)

THIS GROUP OF MASTERS at King Edward VI Grammar School was taken in 1958 by H.L. Howe. The masters are, from left to right, back row: Colin Morgan, Bill Pearce (an Australian music teacher), Dick Neale, David Cooper, Turner, Barr, R.N. Benton and Bernard Teather. Front row, from left to right, are: Rodgerson (the art master), Major Meade, Parkinson, Hemming, Hedley Warr (the headmaster), Foster, Rowlands, Don Brabban and Hobbs.

THE GRAMMAR SCHOOL is not just dependant on academic study. Here we see a group in more light-hearted vein as the cast for a play in February 1956.

LOUTH OPERATIC SOCIETY never got going after the Second World War. This was the first musical production staged by the Louth Playgoers. It was *Salad Days* and the cast included: Percy Wilson, Michael Vincent and Maureen Vincent.

HERE WE SEE two prominent members of the Louth Playgoers from their production of *Posthorn Gallup*. Janet West and Tom Munslow have been stalwarts of the Society in recent years.

ONE OF THE best views of St James' is from Upgate. This view has changed very little despite the building work on the left-hand side of the phtotograph. C.G. Smiths and the Blue Stone Inn may have gone and the Lincolnshire Gun shop is now an Indian restaurant but luckily the proportions of the newly built houses and shops match those in this 1950s photograph.

A GROUP OF Louth Cubs and Guides marching up Eastgate on Mayor's Sunday. Even in the short time since this photograph was taken the Ship & Hounds pub has become a florist's, Fine Fare supermarket a Wilko DIY store and Mike Graves sweetshop on the corner of — Lane a Tip-Top Chemist's store. (Ken Atterby.)

IN THE MAIN Louth and the surrounding area belongs to canny farmers and their affluence. Here is a dispersal sale in Tathwell in 1964. Dick Pridgeon (fourth from the right) is looking over the sheep.

THIS FLOODLIT PHOTOGRAPH of St James' was taken in 1934 at the time of the Silver Jubilee celebrations. There has been a church on this site for over 1,000 years where Ludensians and visitors have worshipped. Aptly dedicated to St James, the patron saint of pilgrims, many people pass through its portals each year.

ACKNOWLEDGEMENTS

In preparing this book I am particularly indebted to the following for lending me photographs and postcards:

Charles Smith • Harold Jackson • Miss Broadley • Lincolnshire Library Service (Victoria Road) • Cecil Simpson (curator, Louth Museum) • David Harrison William Haggas • Joe Law • Mrs Langley • Steve Lee • RN Benton Maple Bedford • Phyllis West • Douglas Matthews • Brian Howe Terry Vamplew • Ernie Bosworth • Jan Tierney (curator, Welholme Galleries) David Sandwith and John Lill.